6TH EDITION

# WORLD HERITAGE SITES

# A FIREFLY BOOK

Published jointly by the United Nations Educational, Scientific and Cultural Organization (UNESCO), 7 place de Fontenoy, 75352 Paris 07 sp, France, and Firefly Books Ltd. 2014

Text © UNESCO 2014
Maps © Collins Bartholomew Ltd 2014
Photographs © as per credits on page 911-12

First printing

**Publisher Cataloging-in-Publication Data (U.S.)**

A CIP record for this title is available from the Library of Congress

**Library and Archives Canada Cataloguing in Publication**

A CIP record for this title is available from Library and Archives Canada

Published in the United States by
Firefly Books (U.S.) Inc.
P.O. Box 1338, Ellicott Station
Buffalo, New York 14205

Published in Canada by
Firefly Books Ltd.
50 Staples Avenue, Unit 1
Richmond Hill, Ontario L4B 0A7

Printed and bound in China

For more information on World Heritage, please contact:
UNESCO World Heritage Centre
7 place de Fontenoy
75352 Paris 07 SP, France
Tel: (33) 01 45 68 15 71
Fax: (33) 01 45 68 55 70
e-mail: wh-info@unesco.org
http://whc.unesco.org

**MIX**
Paper from
responsible sources
FSC www.fsc.org   **FSC® C007454**

FSC™ is a non-profit international organisation established to promote the responsible management of the world's forests. Products carrying the FSC label are independently certified to assure consumers that they come from forests that are managed to meet the social, economic and ecological needs of present and future generations, and other controlled sources.

6TH EDITION

# WORLD HERITAGE SITES

A COMPLETE GUIDE
TO 1007 UNESCO
WORLD HERITAGE SITES

FIREFLY BOOKS

# How to use this book

The page on which the information on a World Heritage site can be found is accessed in a number of ways – by consulting the continent maps on which all the sites are located, or by reference to either the alphabetical or country index. All entries are presented in a similar manner and are arranged chronologically by the year in which they were first inscribed on the World Heritage List.

The diagram below indicates the individual components of each entry and explains the colour coding used to distinguish whether a site is classified as natural, cultural or mixed.

**Site title**
gives the official UNESCO World Heritage title for each entry.

**Red band**
represents entries classified as cultural sites.

**Locator map**
shows the location of the site in a wider region.

**Blue band**
represents entries classified as mixed sites.

**Timeline**
on every page highlights the year in which the sites were first inscribed.

**Site location**
indicates the country where the site can be found.

**Green band**
represents entries classified as natural sites.

Over 650 photographs are included in the book.

**Criteria summary**
To be included on the World Heritage List, sites must be of outstanding universal value and meet at least one out of ten selection criteria. Full criteria explanation can be found on pages **870–1**.

**Main text**
gives concise descriptions and information about each site.

**Extra information**
about each site supplements the details in the main text.

# Contents

# Foreword
by Irina Bokova
Director-General of UNESCO

The World's Heritage provides us with a unique map of the world – a map where the traditional boundaries between States are blurred, that highlights the links binding humanity, and which reveals the intimate relationship between culture and nature, between human genius and natural beauty. The 1972 World Heritage Convention is the foremost international treaty for the protection of major natural and cultural heritage around the world. For four decades, the Convention has helped to safeguard extraordinary places for the enlightenment and enjoyment of future generations.

Today, 981 sites are inscribed on the World Heritage List. Located in 160 countries, they include 759 cultural, 193 natural, and 29 mixed sites – all of which have been recognized for their 'outstanding universal value'. Each site is anchored in a unique cultural and natural context, while being woven into the wider history of humanity and the world, as motifs in the tapestry of a common, irreplaceable heritage.

India's Taj Mahal, the Serengeti in Tanzania, and Machu Picchu in Peru have iconic status. Other World Heritage sites are less well-known – the Old Town of Lijiang, China, whose architecture draws on several cultures over many centuries; the volcanic island of Surtsey in Iceland that was formed in the 1960s; the outstanding ancient rock art of Tsodilo in Botswana; and the 60 active glaciers of the Olympic National Park in the United States of America. The diversity of World Heritage sites is simply astounding. All are there to be discovered anew – starting within these pages, through these maps and striking photographs.

These pages tell also the story of the evolution of the World Heritage Convention itself, with the emergence of new categories of sites. Cultural landscapes record the relationship between nature and culture over time. The Rice Terraces of the Philippines and the Tokaj Wine Region Historic Cultural Landscape in Hungary bear witness to techniques of cultivating land that preserve biodiversity while supporting livelihoods. Other cultural landscapes reveal powerful spiritual bonds between people and their environment, such as the monasteries and the sacred cedar trees of Lebanon's Ouadi Qadisha (the Holy Valley) and the Forest of the Cedars of God (Horsh Arz el-Rab), and the Royal Hill of Ambohimanga in Madagascar. All such sites highlight the creative interaction between communities and the world in which they live.

Recent years have seen the rise of transboundary sites (they number 29 today), located in two or more countries, and jointly nominated and managed. The Wadden Sea in Germany and the Netherlands and the Talamanca Range-La Amistad Reserves / La Amistad National Park in Costa Rica and Panama illustrate this new spirit of collaboration and cooperation.

The inscription of a site is the beginning of a journey. UNESCO works to monitor, provide technical assistance and share knowledge, but ultimate responsibility for conservation lies with States. World Heritage sites can be tremendous vectors for dialogue, development and knowledge. When accommodation, transportation, guiding and business are developed in a sustainable manner, heritage tourism can be extremely beneficial to the site and the communities living in and around it – both socially and economically.

Today's young people are tomorrow's custodians. The World Heritage Centre has launched innovative initiatives to make them aware of the need to preserve heritage and encourage them to take action. Through the Patrimonito cartoons for children and the World Heritage Volunteers programme, it is important that young people are being engaged with early.

Protecting heritage lies at the heart of UNESCO's mandate. It is important for fostering a dialogue among cultures, it is a foundation for reconciliation amongst peoples and it contributes to the sustainable development of societies. In a world of change, world heritage is a reminder of all that unites humanity. I trust this updated edition of The World's Heritage will provide readers with a better understanding of our planet's cultural and bio-diversity, which UNESCO works every day to safeguard for the benefit of all.

*Irina Bokova*

# World Heritage Sites
# Europe

### Belarus
Architectural, Residential and Cultural Complex of the Radziwill Family at Nesvizh p748▼; Belovezhskaya Pushcha / Białowieża Forest p61; Mir Castle Complex p635; Struve Geodetic Arc p747▲.

### Cyprus
Choirokoitia p554▼; Painted Churches in the Troodos Region p210▼; Paphos p101.

### Denmark
Jelling Mounds, Runic Stones and Church p426▼; Ilulissat Icefjord p708 (see map on p15); Kronborg Castle p608; Roskilde Cathedral p452.

### Estonia
Historic Centre (Old Town) of Tallinn p509; Struve Geodetic Arc p747▲.

### Finland
Bronze Age Burial Site of Sammallahdenmäki p599▲; Fortress of Suomenlinna p378; Old Rauma p368▼; High Coast / Kvarken Archipelago p630▲; Petäjävesi Old Church p436▼; Struve Geodetic Arc p747▲; Verla Groundwood and Board Mill p486▼.

### Germany
Aachen Cathedral p33; Abbey and Altenmünster of Lorsch p379▲; Bauhaus and its Sites in Weimar and Dessau p484▲; Bergpark Wilhelmshöhe p866; Berlin Modernism Housing Estates p784▼; Castles of Augustusburg and Falkenlust at Brühl p193▲; Classical Weimar p549; Collegiate Church, Castle and Old Town of Quedlinburg p441▲;

Cologne Cathedral p474; Fagus Factory in Alfeld p826▲; Frontiers of the Roman Empire: Upper German-Raetian Limes p273; Garden Kingdom of Dessau-Wörlitz p610▲; Hanseatic City of Lübeck p281; Historic Centres of Stralsund and Wismar p690▲; Luther Memorials in Eisleben and Wittenberg p503▲; Margravial Opera House Bayreuth p856▲; Maulbronn Monastery Complex p407▼; Messel Pit Fossil Site p456▼; Mines of Rammelsberg and Historic Town of Goslar and Upper Harz Water Management System p387; Monastic Island of Reichenau p640▼; Museumsinsel (Museum Island), Berlin p578; Muskauer Park / Park Muzakowski p719▼; Old town of Regensburg with Stadtamhof p753; Palaces and Parks of Potsdam and Berlin p346; Pilgrimage Church of Wies p176▼; Prehistoric Pile Dwellings around the Alps p839▲; Primeval Beech Forests of the Carpathians and the Ancient Beech Forests of Germany p772; Roman Monuments, Cathedral of St Peter and Church of Our Lady in Trier p251; Speyer Cathedral p128▼; St Mary's Cathedral and St Michael's Church at Hildesheim p225▼; The Wadden Sea p804; Town Hall and Roland on the Marketplace of Bremen p727; Town of Bamberg p406; Upper Middle Rhine Valley p684▼; Völklingen Ironworks p441▼; Wartburg Castle p589; Würzburg Residence with the Court Gardens and Residence Square p132; Zollverein Coal Mine Industrial Complex in Essen p667▼.

continued on page 12

### Key to maps

● Cultural site

● Natural site

● Mixed site

23 Page number reference

▲▼ top/bottom of page

The maps in this section are laid out by geographical continent. Please see the maps on page 872 for UNESCO's regional areas.

232▼

747▲

449▼

497

747▲

716▲

504▼

392▼

449▼

**NORWAY**

742
81

104

630▲  630▲  **FINLAND**

**SWEDEN**

356▲

43

742

847▲

667▲  368▲  599▲

436▼

747▲

486▼

744

643▼

408▲

378

344

383

**RUSSIAN FEDERATION**

432▼

371

404▲ 435▲

509

747▲

**ESTONIA**

725▲

459

646

420  396

804  426▼  608

640▲

544

**LATVIA**

747▲

350

870▲

**DENMARK** 452

553

728  427

804  878

**LITHUANIA**

747▲

804  281  690▲ 690▲

615

715▼

DS

727  503▲  772

**RUS. FED.**

421

871  866 441▲  346

547

635

**BELARUS**

589  826 387 484  610▲

526

748▼

456▼ 484  503▲ 719▲

578

784▼

61

747▲

379▲ 132 549

675▲ 752▲

**POLAND**

61

407▼  856

675▲

89

347

839▲ 406

30

382▲

839▲  753

40  36

868▼

640▼ 176▼

594

702

564

**UKRAINE**

868▼  772  868▼

747▲  827

e large-scale map on pages 10–11

868▼

747▲

865▲

828  226  442

550

870▼  237▼  225▲  292

876▲

**TURKEY**

230

329

856▼

333

**CYPRUS**  210▼

101▲  554▼

Scale 1 : 20 000 000        9

FRANCE

BELGIUM

LUXEMBOURG

SWITZERLAND

AUSTRIA

CZECH REP

SLOVENIA

CROA

ITALY

SAN
MARINO

HOLY
SEE

MONACO

ANDORRA

Corsica
(France)

Sardinia
(Italy)

Sicily
(Italy)

MALTA

B
H

794▼

650
555
745▼ 562▼
562▼ 562▼
850▲ 562▼ 562▼
850▲ 575 562▼ 805▲
794 655▲ 648▲
850▲ 652 554▲ 855▲
738▼ 117 855▼

360
372

62 669
65 113

622

794

169

334

794

153▼ 794
839▲
800▲ 157 839▲ 839▲ 176▲ 498▲ 839▲ 531
839▲ 839▲ 585
777 660 787 159▼
784▲ 610▲ 807 824▲ 839▲
839▲ 704▲ 76▲ 839▲ 565▲ 858▲
839▲ 695▲ 824▲ 839▲ 618 268▲ 261▲
695▲ 824▲ 465 839▲ 839▲ 516▲ 57
541 95 839▲ 532▲
884 695▲ 839▲ 797 453
884 759▲ 520

513
513 860▲ 782▲
265 134 567 627▼
358 460 533
724 495 632
824
824

174

729▼ 729▼ 673
180 92 595
527 824
448▲ 524 506▲
538▲ 399
558▲

546▼

625

86▲
542 546▲ 690▼
690▼ 750▼
690▼ 690▼ 750▼
690▼ 690▼

96
93
98▲

384
392▲
386
64▲
6

384

44▼
557▼
813 826▼ 872▼
229 120
508▼ 480 444
514 131
732▲ 794
794

561
794
794

168▼ 381 66 121▲

794

58

168▼

775 600

# World Heritage Sites
## Europe

**Albania**
Butrint p389; Historic Centres of Berat and Gjirokastra p732▼.

**Andorra**
Madriu-Perafita-Claror Valley p732▲.

**Austria**
City of Graz – Historic Centre and Schloss Eggenberg p585; Fertö / Neusiedlersee Cultural Landscape p664▼; Hallstatt-Dachstein / Salzkammergut Cultural Landscape p531; Historic Centre of the City of Salzburg p498; Historic Centre of Vienna p678; Palace and Gardens of Schönbrunn p502; Prehistoric Pile Dwellings around the Alps p839▲; Semmering Railway p551▲; Wachau Cultural Landscape p641.

**Belgium**
Belfries of Belgium and France p575; Flemish Béguinages p562▼; Historic Centre of Brugge p650; La Grand-Place, Brussels p555; Major Mining Sites of Wallonia p855▼; Major Town Houses of the Architect Victor Horta (Brussels) p648▼; Neolithic Flint Mines at Spiennes (Mons) p652; Notre-Dame Cathedral in Tournai p655▲; Plantin-Moretus House-Workshops-Museum Complex p745▼; Stoclet House p805▲; The Four Lifts on the Canal du Centre and their Environs, La Louvière and Le Roeulx (Hainault) p554▲.

**Bosnia and Herzegovina**
Mehmed Paša Sokolović Bridge in Višegrad p779; Old Bridge Area of the Old City of Mostar p734.

**Bulgaria**
Ancient City of Nessebar p165; Boyana Church p60▼; Madara Rider p69▲; Pirin National Park p179; Rila Monastery p178; Rock-Hewn Churches of Ivanovo p69▼; Srebarna Nature Reserve p168▲; Thracian Tomb of Kazanlak p49▼; Thracian Tomb of Sveshtari p234▲.

**Croatia**
Cathedral of St James in Šibenik p627; Episcopal Complex of the Euphrasian Basilica in the Historic Centre of Poreč p516▼; Historic City of Trogir p533; Historical Complex of Split with the Palace of Diocletian p82; Old City of Dubrovnik p86; Plitvice Lakes National Park p57; Stari Grad Plain p790▼.

**Czech Republic**
Gardens and Castle at Kroměříž p565▼; Historic Centre of Český Krumlov p386; Historic Centre of Prague p384; Historic Centre of Telč p392▲; Holašovice Historical Village Reservation p551▼; Holy Trinity Column in Olomouc p637; Jewish Quarter and St Procopius' Basilica in Třebíč p704▼; Kutná Hora: Historical Town Centre with the Church of St Barbara and the Cathedral of Our Lady at Sedlec p469; Lednice-Valtice Cultural Landscape p493; Litomyšl Castle p588▲; Pilgrimage Church of St John of Nepomuk at Zelená Hora p443; Tugendhat Villa in Brno p681▼.

continued on page 13

Scale 1 : 10 000 000    11

# Europe (continued from page 8)

**Iceland**
Surtsey p789▼; Þingvellir National Park p709.

**Ireland**
Brú na Bóinne – Archaeological Ensemble of the Bend of the Boyne p401▲; Skellig Michael Monastery p492.

**Latvia**
Historic Centre of Riga p544; Struve Geodetic Arc p747▲.

**Lithuania**
Curonian Spit p615; Kernavė Archaeological Site (Cultural Reserve of Kernavė) p715▼; Struve Geodetic Arc p747▲; Vilnius Historic Centre p421.

**Netherlands**
Defence Line of Amsterdam p488; Droogmakerij de Beemster (Beemster Polder) p580; Historic Area of Willemstad, Inner City and Harbour, Curaçao p528▼ (see map p16); Ir. D.F. Woudagemaal (D.F. Wouda Steam Pumping Station) p566; Mill Network at Kinderdijk-Elshout p523; Rietveld Schröderhuis (Rietveld Schröder House) p636▲; Schokland and Surroundings p449▲; Seventeenth-century canal ring area of Amsterdam inside the Singelgracht p818; The Wadden Sea p804.

**Norway**
Bryggen p43; Rock Art of Alta p232▼; Røros Mining Town and the Circumference p104; Struve Geodetic Arc p747▲; Urnes Stave Church p81; Vegaøyan – the Vega Archipelago p716▲; West Norwegian Fjords – Geirangerfjord and Nærøyfjord p742.

**Poland**
Auschwitz Birkenau German Nazi Concentration and Extermination Camp (1940-1945) p40; Castle of the Teutonic Order in Malbork p547; Centennial Hall in Wrocław p752▲; Belovezhskaya Pushcha / Białowieża Forest p61; Churches of Peace in Jawor and Swidnica p675▲; Historic Centre of Kraków p30; Historic Centre of Warsaw p89; Kalwaria Zebrzydowska: the Mannerist Architectural and Park Landscape Complex and Pilgrimage Park p594; Medieval Town of Toruń p526; Muskauer Park / Park Muzakowski p719▼; Old City of Zamość p382▼; Wieliczka and Bochnia Royal Salt Mines p36; Wooden Churches of Southern Małopolska p702; Wooden Tserkvas of the Carpathian Region in Poland and Ukraine p868▼.

**Portugal**
Alto Douro Wine Region p662; Central Zone of the Town of Angra do Heroismo in the Azores p162▼; Convent of Christ in Tomar p175; Cultural Landscape of Sintra p447; Garrison Border Town of Elvas and its Fortifications p851; Historic Centre of Évora p258; Historic Centre of Guimarães p24; Historic Centre of Oporto p482; Landscape of the Pico Island Vineyard Culture p731; Laurisilva of Madeira p602; Monastery of Alcobaça p337; Monastery of Batalha p177; Monastery of the Hieronymites and

Tower of Belém in Lisbon p163; Prehistoric Rock-Art Sites in the Côa Valley and Siega Verde p563▼; University of Coimbra – Alta and Sofia p863▲.

**Russian Federation** (see also p24)
Architectural Ensemble of the Trinity Sergius Laura in Sergiev Posad p420; Church of the Ascension, Kolomenskoye p427; Cultural and Historic Ensemble of the Solovetsky Islands p392▼; Curonian Spit p615; Ensemble of the Ferrapontov Monastery p643▼; Ensemble of the Novodevichy Convent p728; Historic and Architectural Complex of the Kazan Kremlin p646; Historic Centre of Saint Petersburg and Related Groups of Monuments p344; Historic Monuments of Novgorod and Surroundings p383; Historical Centre of the City of Yaroslavl p744; Kizhi Pogost p356▲; Kremlin and Red Square, Moscow p350; Struve Geodetic Arc p747▲; Virgin Komi Forests p449▼; White Monuments of Vladimir and Suzdal p396.

**Spain**
Alhambra, Generalife and Albayzín, Granada p202; Aranjuez Cultural Landscape p658▼; Archaeological Ensemble of Mérida p410; Archaeological Ensemble of Tárraco p621▼; Archaeological Site of Atapuerca p647▲; Burgos Cathedral p200; Catalan Romanesque Churches of the Vall de Boí p644▲; Cathedral, Alcázar and Archivo de Indias in Seville p266; Cave of Altamira and Paleolithic Cave Art of Northern Spain p220▲; Cultural Landscape of the Serra de Tramuntana p839▼; Doñana National Park p430▲; Garajonay National Park p250▲; Heritage of Mercury: Almadén p858▲; Historic Centre of Cordoba p198; Historic City of Toledo p242; Historic Walled Town of Cuenca p505; Ibiza, Biodiversity and Culture p572; La Lonja de la Seda de Valencia p485▲; Las Médulas p535▲; Monastery and Site of the Escurial, Madrid p193▼; Monuments of Oviedo and the Kingdom of the Asturias p217; Mudéjar Architecture of Aragon p256; Old City of Salamanca p328; Old Town of Ávila with its Extra-Muros Churches p233; Old Town of Cáceres p253; Old Town of Segovia and its Aqueduct p209; Palau de la Música Catalana and Hospital de Sant Pau, Barcelona p528▲; Palmeral of Elche p639; Poblet Monastery p366; Prehistoric Rock-Art Sites in the Côa Valley and Siega Verde p563▼; Pyrénées - Mont Perdu p508▼; Renaissance Monumental Ensembles of Úbeda and Baeza p697▼; Rock Art of the Mediterranean Basin on the Iberian Peninsula p562▲; Roman Walls of Lugo p649▲; Route of Santiago de Compostela p397; Royal Monastery of Santa María de Guadalupe p416▲; San Cristóbal de La Laguna p587▼; San Millán Yuso and Suso Monasteries p535▼; Santiago de Compostela (Old Town) p211; Teide National Park p766; University and Historic Precinct of Alcalá de Henares p568; Tower of Hercules p806; Vizcaya Bridge p758; Works of Antoni Gaudí p182.

**Sweden**
Agricultural Landscape of Southern Öland p640▲;

Birka and Hovgården p404▲; Church Village of Gammelstad, Luleå p504▼; ); Decorated Farmhouses of Hälsingland p847▲; Engelsberg Ironworks p408▲; Hanseatic Town of Visby p459; High Coast / Kvarken Archipelago p630▲; Laponian Area p497; Mining Area of the Great Copper Mountain in Falun p667▲; Naval Port of Karlskrona p553; Rock Carvings in Tanum p432▼; Royal Domain of Drottningholm p371; Skogskyrkogården p435▲; Struve Geodetic Arc p747▲; Varberg Radio Station p725▲.

**Turkey**
Archaeological Site of Troy p550; City of Safranbolu p442; Göreme National Park and the Rock Sites of Cappadocia p230; Great Mosque and Hospital of Divriği p225▲; Hattusha: the Hittite Capital p237▼; Hierapolis-Pamukkale p329; Historic Areas of Istanbul p226; Nemrut Dağ p292; Neolithic Site of Çatalhöyük p856▼; Selimiye Mosque and its Social Complex p828; Xanthos-Letoon p333▼.

**Ukraine**
Ancient City of Tauric Chersonese and its Chora p865▲; Kiev: Saint-Sophia Cathedral and Related Monastic Buildings, Kiev-Pechersk Laura p347; L'viv – the Ensemble of the Historic Centre p564; Primeval Beech Forests of the Carpathians and the Ancient Beech Forests of Germany p772; Residence of Bukovinian and Dalmatia Metropolitans p827; Struve Geodetic Arc p747▲; Wooden Tserkvas of the Carpathian Region in Poland and Ukraine p868▼.

**United Kingdom**
Blaenavon Industrial Landscape p620▼; Blenheim Palace p270; Canterbury Cathedral, St Augustine's Abbey and St Martin's Church p327; Castles and Town Walls of King Edward in Gwynedd p257▼; City of Bath p290; Cornwall and West Devon Mining Landscape p757; Derwent Valley Mills p675▼; Dorset and East Devon Coast p671; Durham Castle and Cathedral p246; Frontiers of the Roman Empire: Antonine Wall and Hadrian's Wall p273; Giant's Causeway and Causeway Coast p244; Gough and Inaccessible Islands p468▼ (see map on p18); Heart of Neolithic Orkney p570; Henderson Island p321▼ (see map p21); Historic Town of St George and Related Fortifications, Bermuda p621▲ (see map on p15); Ironbridge Gorge p239; Liverpool – Maritime Mercantile City p707▼; Maritime Greenwich p507; New Lanark p659; Old and New Towns of Edinburgh p470; Palace of Westminster and Westminster Abbey including Saint Margaret's Church p272; Pontcysyllte Aqueduct and Canal p801; Royal Botanic Gardens, Kew p692; Saltaire p665; St Kilda p241; Stonehenge, Avebury and Associated Sites p254; Studley Royal Park including the Ruins of Fountains Abbey p248; Tower of London p312.

# Europe (continued from page 11)

**France**

Abbey Church of Saint-Savin sur Gartempe p168▼; Amiens Cathedral p117; Arles, Roman and Romanesque Monuments p131; Belfries of Belgium and France p575; Bordeaux, Port of the Moon p775; Bourges Cathedral p381; Canal du Midi p480; Cathedral of Notre-Dame, Former Abbey of Saint-Rémi and Palace of Tau, Reims p372; Chartres Cathedral p65; Cistercian Abbey of Fontenay p121▲; Episcopal City of Albi p813; Fortifications of Vauban p794; From the Great Saltworks of Salins-les-Bains to the Royal Saltworks of Arc-et-Senans, the production of open-pan salt p153▲; Gulf of Porto: Calanche of Piana, Gulf of Girolata, Scandola Reserve p174; Historic Centre of Avignon: Papal Palace, Episcopal Ensemble and Avignon Bridge p444; Historic Fortified City of Carcassonne p514; Historic Site of Lyons p561; Jurisdiction of Saint-Emilion p600; Lagoons of New Caledonia: Reef Diversity and Associated Ecosystems p788▼ (see map on page 21); Le Havre, the city rebuilt by Auguste Perret p738▲; Mont-Saint-Michel and its Bay p58; Nord–Pas de Calais Mining Basin p850▲; Palace and Park of Fontainebleau p113; Palace and Park of Versailles p62; Paris, Banks of the Seine p360; Pitons, cirques and remparts of Reunion Island p812 (see map on page 18); Place Stanislas, Place de la Carrière and Place d'Alliance in Nancy p169; Pont du Gard (Roman Aqueduct) p229; Prehistoric Pile Dwellings around the Alps p839▲; Prehistoric Sites and Decorated Caves of the Vézère Valley p44▼; Provins, Town of Medieval Fairs p669; Pyrénées - Mont Perdu p508▼; Roman Theatre and its Surroundings and the 'Triumphal Arch' of Orange p120; Routes of Santiago de Compostela in France p557▼; Strasbourg – Grande île p334; The Causses and the Cévennes, Mediterranean agro-pastoral Cultural Landscape p826▼; The Loire Valley between Sully-sur-Loire and Chalonnes p622; Vézelay, Church and Hill p66.

**Greece**

Acropolis, Athens p282; Archaeological Site of Aigai (modern name Vergina) p504▲; Archaeological Site of Delphi p262; Archaeological Site of Mystras p341; Archaeological Site of Olympia p336; Archaeological Sites of Mycenae and Tiryns p574; Delos p353; Historic Centre (Chorá) with the Monastery of Saint John, the Theologian, and the Cave of the Apocalypse on the Island of Pátmos p603; Medieval City of Rhodes p324; Meteora p332; Monasteries of Daphni, Hosios Loukas and Nea Moni of Chios p342▼; Mount Athos p309; Old Town of Corfu p771; Paleochristian and Byzantine Monuments of Thessalonika p313▼; Pythagoreion and Heraion of Samos p388▼; Sanctuary of Asklepios at Epidaurus p315; Temple of Apollo Epicurius at Bassae p240▼.

**Holy See**

Historic Centre of Rome, the Properties of the Holy See in that City Enjoying Extraterritorial Rights and San Paolo Fuori le Mura p92; Vatican City p180.

**Hungary**

Budapest, including the Banks of the Danube, the Buda Castle Quarter and Andrássy Avenue p274; Caves of Aggtelek Karst and Slovak Karst p456▲; Early Christian Necropolis of Pécs (Sopianae) p619▼; Fertő / Neusiedlersee Cultural Landscape p664▼; Hortobágy National Park - the Puszta p583▼; Millenary Benedictine Abbey of Pannonhalma and its Natural Environment p479; Old Village of Hollókő and its Surroundings p293; Tokaj Wine Region Historic Cultural Landscape p686.

**Italy**

Archaeological Area and the Patriarchal Basilica of Aquileia p565▲; Archaeological Area of Agrigento p542; Archaeological Areas of Pompei, Herculaneum and Torre Annunziata p524; Assisi, the Basilica of San Francesco and Other Franciscan Sites p632; Botanical Garden (Orto Botanico), Padua p532▲; Castel del Monte p506▲; Cathedral, Torre Civica and Piazza Grande, Modena p520, Church and Dominican Convent of Santa Maria delle Grazie with 'The Last Supper' by Leonardo da Vinci p95; Cilento and Vallo di Diano National Park with the Archeological sites of Paestum and Velia, and the Certosa di Padula p558▲; City of Verona p618; City of Vicenza and the Palladian Villas of the Veneto p428; Costiera Amalfitana p538; Crespi d'Adda p465; Early Christian Monuments of Ravenna p487; Eighteenth-Century Royal Palace at Caserta with the Park, the Aqueduct of Vanvitelli, and the San Leucio Complex p527; Etruscan Necropolises of Cerveteri and Tarquinia p729▼; Ferrara, City of the Renaissance, and its Po Delta p453; Genoa: Le Strade Nuove and the system of the Palazzi dei Rolli p759▲; Historic Centre of Florence p134; Historic Centre of Naples p448; Historic Centre of Rome, the Properties of the Holy See in that City Enjoying Extraterritorial Rights and San Paolo Fuori le Mura p92; Historic Centre of San Gimignano p358; Historic Centre of Siena p460; Historic Centre of the City of Pienza p495; Historic Centre of Urbino p567; Isole Eolie (Aeolian Islands) p625; Late Baroque Towns of the Val di Noto (South-Eastern Sicily) p690▼; Longobards in Italy. Places of the power (568-774 AD) p824; Mantua and Sabbioneta p797; Medici Villas and Gardens in Tuscany p860▲; Monte San Giorgio p704▲; Mount Etna p869▲; Piazza del Duomo, Pisa p265; Portovenere, Cinque Terre, and the Islands (Palmaria, Tino and Tinetto) p513; Prehistoric Pile Dwellings around the Alps p839▲; Residences of the Royal House of Savoy p541; Rhaetian Railway in the Albula / Bernina Landscapes p784▲; Rock Drawings in Valcamonica p76▲; Sacri Monti of Piedmont and Lombardy p695▲; Su Nuraxi di Barumini p546▼; Syracuse and the Rocky Necropolis of Pantalica p750▼; The Dolomites p807; The Sassi and the park of the Rupestrian Churches of Matera p399;

The Trulli of Alberobello p501; Val d'Orcia p724; Venice and its Lagoon p268; Villa Adriana (Tivoli) p595; Villa d'Este, Tivoli p673; Villa Romana del Casale p546▲.

**Luxembourg**

City of Luxembourg: its Old Quarters and Fortifications p424.

**Malta**

City of Valletta p93; Hal Saflieni Hypogeum p98▲; Megalithic Temples of Malta p96.

**Montenegro**

Durmitor National Park p107; Natural and Culturo-Historical Region of Kotor p84.

**Republic of Moldova**

Struve Geodetic Arc p747▲.

**Romania**

Churches of Moldavia p412▲; Dacian Fortresses of the Orastie Mountains p597; Danube Delta p362; Historic Centre of Sighişoara p592; Monastery of Horezu p408▼; Villages with Fortified Churches in Transylvania p404▼; Wooden Churches of Maramureş p581.

**San Marino**

San Marino Historic Centre and Mount Titano p782.

**Serbia**

Gamzigrad-Romuliana, Palace of Galerius p776; Medieval Monuments in Kosovo p717▼; Stari Ras and Sopoćani p76▼; Studenica Monastery p250▼.

**Slovakia**

Bardejov Town Conservation Reserve p645; Caves of Aggtelek Karst and Slovak Karst p456▲; Historic Town of Banská Štiavnica and the Technical Monuments in its Vicinity p414; Levoča, Spišský Hrad and the Associated Cultural Monuments p417; Primeval Beech Forests of the Carpathians and the Ancient Beech Forests of Germany p772; Vlkolínec p418; Wooden Churches of the Slovak part of the Carpathian Mountain Area p795▲.

**Slovenia**

Heritage of Mercury: Idrija p858▲; Prehistoric Pile Dwellings around the Alps p839▲; Škocjan Caves p261▲.

**Switzerland**

Abbey of St Gall p176▲; Benedictine Convent of St John at Müstair p159▼; La Chaux-de-Fonds / Le Locle, Watchmaking Town Planning p800▲; Lavaux, Vineyard Terraces p777; Monte San Giorgio p704▲; Old City of Berne p157; Prehistoric Pile Dwellings around the Alps p839▲; Rhaetian Railway in the Albula/Bernina Landscapes p784▲; Swiss Alps Jungfrau-Aletsch p660; Swiss Tectonic Arena Sardona p787;Three Castles, Defensive Wall and Ramparts of the Market-Town of Bellinzone p610▼.

**The former Yugoslav Republic of Macedonia**

Natural and Cultural Heritage of the Ohrid Region p77.

# World Heritage Sites
## North America and the Caribbean

**Barbados**
Historic Bridgetown and its Garrison p829▲.

**Belize**
Belize Barrier Reef Reserve System p483.

**Canada**
Canadian Rocky Mountain Parks p194; Dinosaur Provincial Park p48; Gros Morne National Park p302; Head-Smashed-In Buffalo Jump p118▲; Historic District of Old Québec p206; Joggins Fossil Cliffs p796▲; Kluane / Wrangell-St Elias / Glacier Bay / Tatshenshini-Alsek p52; Landscape of Grand Pré p849▲; L'Anse aux Meadows National Historic Site p37▼; Miguasha National Park p599▼; Nahanni National Park p38▲; Old Town Lunenburg p463; Red Bay Basque Whaling Station p865▼; Rideau Canal p773; SGang Gwaay p133▲; Waterton Glacier International Peace Park p450; Wood Buffalo National Park p170.

**Costa Rica**
Area de Conservación Guanacaste p596▼; Cocos Island National Park p516▲; Talamanca Range-La Amistad Reserves / La Amistad National Park p162▲.

**Cuba**
Alejandro de Humboldt National Park p672▲; Archaeological Landscape of the First Coffee Plantations in the South-East of Cuba p649▼; Desembarco del Granma National Park p583▲; Historic Centre of Camagüey p785▼; Old Havana and its Fortification System p146; San Pedro de la Roca Castle, Santiago de Cuba p548▲; Trinidad and the Valley de los Ingenios p323; Urban Historic Centre of Cienfuegos p749; Viñales Valley p593▼.

**Dominica**
Morne Trois Pitons National Park p515.

**Dominican Republic**
Colonial City of Santo Domingo p343.

**El Salvador**
Joya de Cerén Archaeological Site p416▼.

**Guatemala**
Antigua Guatemala p73; Archaeological Park and Ruins of Quirigua p130▼; Tikal National Park p88▼.

**Haiti**
National History Park – Citadel, Sans Souci, Ramiers p139▲.

**Honduras**
Maya Site of Copán p90; Río Plátano Biosphere Reserve p142▼.

**Mexico**
Agave Landscape and Ancient Industrial Facilities of Tequila p754; Ancient Maya City of Calakmul, Campeche p687▲; Archaeological Monuments Zone of Xochicalco p605; Archeological Zone of Paquimé, Casas Grandes p563▲; Camino Real de Tierra Adentro p816▼; Central University City Campus of the Universidad Nacional Autónoma de México (UNAM) p770▲; Earliest 16th-Century Monasteries on the Slopes of Popocatepetl p432▲; El Pinacate and Gran Desierto de Altar Biosphere Reserve p864▼; El Tajin, Pre-Hispanic City p394; Franciscan Missions in the Sierra Gorda of Querétaro p703▲; Historic Centre of Mexico City and Xochimilco p284▲; Historic Centre of Morelia p369; Historic Centre of Oaxaca and Archaeological Site of Monte Albán p286; Historic Centre of Puebla p284▼; Historic Centre of Zacatecas p419▲; Historic Fortified Town of Campeche p577; Historic Monuments Zone of Querétaro p496; Historic Monuments Zone of Tlacotalpan p548▼; Historic Town of Guanajuato and Adjacent Mines p318; Hospicio Cabañas, Guadalajara p534; Islands and Protected Areas of the Gulf of California p733; Luis Barragán House and Studio p722▲; Monarch Butterfly Biosphere Reserve p791; Pre-Hispanic City and National Park of Palenque p299; Pre-Hispanic City of Chichen-Itza p330; Pre-Hispanic City of Teotihuacan p288; Pre-Hispanic Town of Uxmal p489; Prehistoric Caves of Yagul and Mitla in the Central Valley of Oaxaca p817▲; Protective town of San Miguel and the Sanctuary of Jesús Nazareno de Atotonilco p781▼; Rock Paintings of the Sierra de San Francisco p419▼; Sian Ka'an p267; Whale Sanctuary of El Vizcaino p401▼.

**Nicaragua**
León Cathedral p829▼; Ruins of León Viejo p619▲.

**Panama**
Archaeological Site of Panamá Viejo and Historic District of Panamá p529; Coiba National Park and its Special Zone of Marine Protection p745▲; Darien National Park p130▲; Fortifications on the Caribbean Side of Panama: Portobelo-San Lorenzo p99; Talamanca Range-La Amistad Reserves / La Amistad National Park p162▲.

**Saint Kitts and Nevis**
Brimstone Hill Fortress National Park p596.

**Saint Lucia**
Pitons Management Area p711.

**United States of America**
Cahokia Mounds State Historic Site p151▲; Carlsbad Caverns National Park p446; Chaco Culture p285; Everglades National Park p53; Grand Canyon National Park p54; Great Smoky Mountains National Park p164; Hawaii Volcanoes National Park p264; Independence Hall p64; La Fortaleza and San Juan National Historic Site in Puerto Rico p166; Kluane / Wrangell-St Elias / Glacier Bay / Tatshenshini-Alsek p52; Mammoth Cave National Park p126▲; Mesa Verde National Park p28; Monticello and the University of Virginia in Charlottesville p304; Olympic National Park p128▲; Papahānaumokuākea p814▼; Redwood National Park p103; Statue of Liberty p187; Taos Pueblo p380▲; Waterton Glacier International Peace Park p450; Yellowstone National Park p34; Yosemite National Park p184▼.

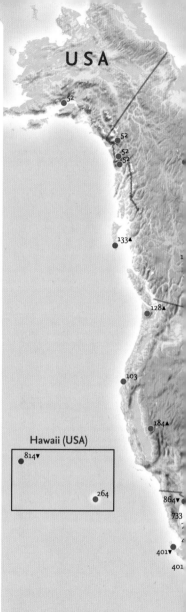

USA

Hawaii (USA)

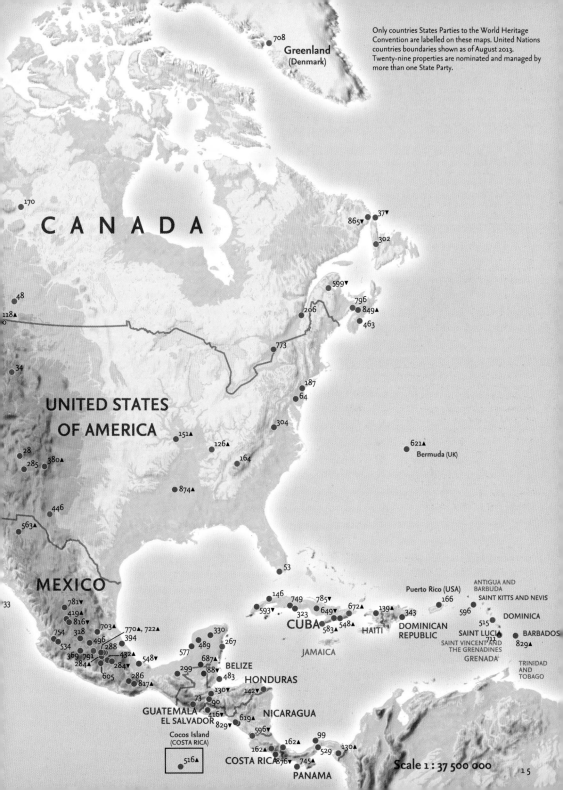

Only countries States Parties to the World Heritage
Convention are labelled on these maps. United Nations
countries boundaries shown as of August 2013.
Twenty-nine properties are nominated and managed by
more than one State Party.

708
Greenland
(Denmark)

CANADA

170

865▼  37▼
302

48
118▲
○

599▼
796
849▲
206
463

34

773

UNITED STATES
OF AMERICA

187
64

304

151▲
126▲
164

621▲
Bermuda (UK)

28
285  380▲

874▲

446

563▲

53

MEXICO

33

146
749
593▼  323  785▼
649▼
672▲  139▲
583▲  548▲
343
HAITI

Puerto Rico (USA)
166
596
515
711
829▲

ANTIGUA AND
BARBUDA
SAINT KITTS AND NEVIS
DOMINICA
SAINT LUCIA
BARBADOS

781▼
419▲
816▼
754  318  703▲  770▲, 722▲
534  496  394
369  791  288  432▲
284▲  284▼  548▼
605
286
817▲

330
489  267
577  687▲
299  88▲
483
130▲  142▲

BELIZE
HONDURAS

CUBA

JAMAICA

DOMINICAN
REPUBLIC

SAINT VINCENT AND
THE GRENADINES
GRENADA

TRINIDAD
AND
TOBAGO

73
116▼
829▼

90
619▲

NICARAGUA

GUATEMALA
EL SALVADOR

Cocos Island
(COSTA RICA)

516▲

596▲
162▲
162▲  876▼

99
529

130▲

745▲

Scale 1 : 37 500 000

COSTA RICA
PANAMA

1 5

528▼ Curaçao (Netherlands)
398▼  644▲
184▼
473▼
426▲

VENEZUELA

431  GUYANA
687▼
658▲
SURINAME

841▼
756▼  COLOMBIA
877▼  473▼
458
32▼
171▲
ECUADOR
576▼

624
537
668▲

356▼
238
214▲
210▲
800▼  326
PERU
296
172▼  877▼
158
434
617
634  BOLIVIA
877▼
877▼  367▲
736  289
556▼
348▲
656
636▼
681▲
674  280
681▲
588▼
588▼
223  108
606
844

Galápagos Islands
(Ecuador)
26

Rapa Nui (Chile)
454

CHILE
877▼
795
PARAGUAY
235
188▲
407▲
159▲  159▲

606

374▲
15▲
809▼
208
579▼
579▼

628
628
647▼

696▲
762▲

URUGUAY
472

ARGENTINA

620▲
590

607▲

111

Only countries States Parties to the World Heritage
Convention are labelled on these maps. United Nations
countries boundaries shown as of August 2013.
Twenty-nine properties are nominated and managed by
more than one State Party.

Scale 1 : 37 000 000

# World Heritage Sites
## South America

### Argentina
Cueva de las Manos, Río Pinturas p607▲; Iguazu National Park p188; Ischigualasto / Talampaya Natural Parks p628; Jesuit Block and Estancias of Córdoba p647▼; Jesuit Missions of the Guaranis: San Ignacio Miní, Santa Ana, Nuestra Señora de Loreto and Santa María Mayor (Argentina), Ruins of Saõ Miguel das Missões (Brazil) p159▲; Parque Nacional Los Glaciares p111; Península Valdés p590; Quebrada de Humahuaca p705.

### Bolivia
City of Potosí p289; Fuerte de Samaipata p556▼; Historic City of Sucre p367▲; Jesuit Missions of the Chiquitos p348▲; Noel Kempff Mercado National Park p636▼; Tiwanaku: Spiritual and Political Centre of the Tiwanaku Culture p634.

### Brazil
Atlantic Forest South-East Reserves p606; Brasilia p280; Brazilian Atlantic Islands: Fernando de Noronha and Atol das Rocas Reserves p668▲; Central Amazon Conservation Complex p624; Cerrado Protected Areas: Chapada dos Veadeiros and Emas National Parks p681▲; Discovery Coast Atlantic Forest Reserves p579▼; Historic Centre of Salvador de Bahia p208; Historic Centre of São Luís p537; Historic Centre of the Town of Diamantina p588▼; Historic Centre of the Town of Goiás p674; Historic Centre of the Town of Olinda p150; Historic Town of Ouro Preto p108; Iguaçu National Park p235; Jesuit Missions of the Guaranis: San Ignacio Miní, Santa Ana, Nuestra Señora de Loreto and Santa María Mayor (Argentina), Ruins of Saõ Miguel das Missões (Brazil) p159▲; Pantanal Conservation Area p656; Rio de Janeiro: Carioca Landscapes between the Mountain and the Sea p844; Sanctuary of Bom Jesus do Congonhas p223; São Francisco Square in the Town of São Cristóvão p809▲; Serra da Capivara National Park p374▲.

### Chile
Churches of Chiloé p620▲; Historic Quarter of the Seaport City of Valparaíso p696▲; Humberstone and Santa Laura Saltpeter Works p736; Rapa Nui National Park p454; Sewell Mining Town p762▲.

### Colombia
Coffee Cultural Landscape of Colombia p841▼; Historic Centre of Santa Cruz de Mompox p473▲; Los Katíos National Park p426▲; Malpelo Fauna and Flora Sanctuary p756▼; National Archeological Park of Tierradentro p473▼; Port, Fortresses and Group of Monuments, Cartagena p184▼; San Agustín Archeological Park p458.

### Ecuador
City of Quito p32▼; Galápagos Islands p26; Historic Centre of Santa Ana de los Ríos de Cuenca p576▼; Sangay National Park p171▲.

### Paraguay
Jesuit Missions of La Santísima Trinidad de Paraná and Jesús de Tavarangue p407▲.

### Peru
Chan Chan Archaeological Zone p238; Chavín (Archaeological site) p210▲; City of Cuzco p158; Historic Centre of Lima p326; Historic Sanctuary of Machu Picchu p172; Historical Centre of the City of Arequipa p617; Huascarán National Park p214; Lines and Geoglyphs of Nasca and Pampas de Jumana p434; Manú National Park p296; Río Abiseo National Park p356▼; Sacred City of Caral-Supe p800.

### Suriname
Central Suriname Nature Reserve p658▲; Historic Inner City of Paramaribo p687▼.

### Uruguay
Historic Quarter of the City of Colonia del Sacramento p472.

### Venezuela
Canaima National Park p431; Ciudad Universitaria de Caracas p644▲; Coro and its Port p398▼.

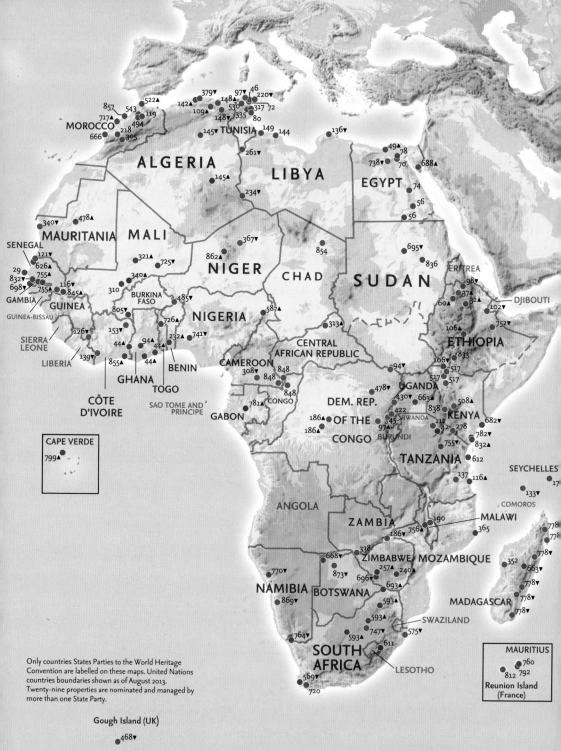

Only countries States Parties to the World Heritage Convention are labelled on these maps. United Nations countries boundaries shown as of August 2013. Twenty-nine properties are nominated and managed by more than one State Party.

Scale 1 : 50 000 000

# World Heritage Sites
## Africa

**Algeria**
Al Qal'a of Beni Hammad p109▲; Djémila p148▲; Kasbah of Algiers p379▼; M'Zab Valley p145▼; Tassili n'Ajjer p145▲; Timgad p148▼; Tipasa p142▲.

**Benin**
Royal Palaces of Abomey p232▲.

**Botswana**
Tsodilo p668▼.

**Burkina Faso**
The Ruins of Loropéni p805▼.

**Cameroon**
Dja Faunal Reserve p308▼; Sangha Trinational p848.

**Cape Verde**
Cidade Velha, Historic Centre of Ribeira Grande p799▲.

**Central African Republic**
Manovo-Gounda St Floris National Park p313▲; Sangha Trinational p848.

**Chad**
Lakes of Ounianga p854.

**Congo**
Sangha Trinational p848.

**Congo, Democratic Republic of the**
Garamba National Park p94▼; Kahuzi-Biega National Park p97▲; Okapi Wildlife Reserve p478▼; Salonga National Park p186▲; Virunga National Park p45.

**Côte d'Ivoire**
Comoé National Park p153▼; Historic Town of Grand-Bassam p855▲; Mount Nimba Strict Nature Reserve p126▼; Taï National Park p139▼.

**Egypt**
Abu Mena p49▲; Ancient Thebes with its Necropolis p74; Historic Cairo p78; Memphis and its Necropolis – the Pyramid Fields from Giza to Dahshur p70; Nubian Monuments from Abu Simbel to Philae p56; Saint Catherine Area p688▲; Wadi Al-Hitan (Whale Valley) p738▼.

**Ethiopia**
Aksum p98▼; Fasil Ghebbi, Gondar Region p60▲; Harar Jugol, the Fortified Historic Town p752▼; Konso Cultural Landscape p833; Lower Valley of the Awash p102▼; Lower Valley of the Omo p106▼; Rock-Hewn Churches, Lalibela p32▲; Simien National Park p37▲; Tiya p106▲.

**Gabon**
Ecosystem and Relict Cultural Landscape of Lopé-Okanda p781▲.

**Gambia**
Kunta Kinteh Island and Related Sites p698▼; Stone Circles of Senegambia p755▲.

**Ghana**
Asante Traditional Buildings p94▲; Forts and Castles, Volta, Greater Accra, Central and Western Regions p44▲.

**Guinea**
Mount Nimba Strict Nature Reserve p126▼.

**Kenya**
Fort Jesus, Mombasa p832▲; Lake Turkana National Parks p517; Lamu Old Town p682▼; Mount Kenya National Park/Natural Forest p508▲; Kenya Lake System in the Great Rift Valley p838; Sacred Mijikenda Kaya Forests p782▼.

**Lesotho**
Maloti-Drakensberg Park p611.

**Libya**
Archaeological Site of Cyrene p136▼; Archaeological Site of Leptis Magna p144; Archaeological Site of Sabratha p149; Old Town of Ghadamès p261▼; Rock-Art Sites of Tadrart Acacus p234▼.

**Madagascar**
Rainforests of the Atsinanana p778▼; The Royal Hill of Ambohimanga p663▼; Tsingy de Bemaraha Strict Nature Reserve p352.

**Malawi**
Chongoni Rock-Art Area p756▲; Lake Malawi National Park p190.

**Mali**
Cliff of Bandiagara (Land of the Dogons) p340▲; Old Towns of Djenné p310; Timbuktu p321▲; Tomb of Askia p725▼.

**Mauritania**
Ancient Ksour of Ouadane, Chinguetti, Tichitt and Oualata p478▲; Banc d'Arguin National Park p340▼.

**Mauritius**
Aapravasi Ghat p760▼; Le Morne Cultural Landscape p792▲.

**Morocco**
Archaeological Site of Volubilis p543; Historic City of Meknes p494; Ksar of Aït-Ben-Haddou p305; Medina of Essaouira (formerly Mogador) p666; Medina of Fez p119; Medina of Marrakesh p218; Medina of Tétouan (formerly known as Titawin) p522▼; Portuguese City of Mazagan (El Jadida) p717▲; Rabat, Modern Capital and Historic City: a Shared Heritage p857.

**Mozambique**
Island of Mozambique p365.

**Namibia**
Namib Sand Sea p869▼; Twyfelfontein or /Ui-//aes p770▼.

**Niger**
Aïr and Ténéré Natural Reserves p367▼; Historic

Centre of Agadez p862▲; W National Park of Niger p485▼.

**Nigeria**
Osun-Osogbo Sacred Grove p741▼; Sukur Cultural Landscape p587▲.

**Senegal**
Bassari Country: Bassari, Fula and Bedik Cultural Landscapes p845▲; Djoudj National Bird Sanctuary p121▼; Island of Gorée p29; Island of Saint-Louis p626▲; Niokolo-Koba National Park p116▼; Saloum Delta p832▼; Stone Circles of Senegambia p755▲.

**Seychelles**
Aldabra Atoll p133▼; Vallée de Mai Nature Reserve p171▼.

**South Africa**
Cape Floral Region Protected Areas p720; Fossil Hominid Sites of South Africa p593▲; iSimangaliso Wetland Park p575▼; Maloti-Drakensberg Park p611; Mapungubwe Cultural Landscape p693▲; Richtersveld Cultural and Botanical Landscape p764▼; Robben Island p569▼; Vredefort Dome p747▼.

**Sudan**
Archaeological Sites of the Island of Meroe p836; Gebel Barkal and the Sites of the Napatan Region p695▼.

**Tanzania**
Kilimanjaro National Park p278; Kondoa Rock-Art Sites p755▼; Ngorongoro Conservation Area p42; Ruins of Kilwa Kisiwani and Ruins of Songo Mnara p116▲; Selous Game Reserve p137; Serengeti National Park p112; Stone Town of Zanzibar p612.

**Togo**
Koutammakou, the Land of the Batammariba p726▲.

**Tunisia**
Amphitheatre of El Jem p80; Dougga / Thugga p530; Ichkeul National Park p97▼; Kairouan p335; Medina of Sousse p317; Medina of Tunis p72; Punic Town of Kerkuane and its Necropolis p220▼; Site of Carthage p46.

**Uganda**
Bwindi Impenetrable National Park p422; Rwenzori Mountains National Park p430▼; Tombs of Buganda Kings at Kasubi p663▲.

**Zambia**
Mosi-oa-Tunya / Victoria Falls p338.

**Zimbabwe**
Great Zimbabwe National Monument p240▲; Khami Ruins National Monument p257▲; Mana Pools National Park, Sapi and Chewore Safari Areas p186▲; Mosi-oa-Tunya / Victoria Falls p338; Matobo Hills p696▲.

PALAU

858▼

786▲

PAPUA
NEW GUINEA

127

311

699

429▼

122

AUSTRALIA

830

306

368▲

260

125

609

763

808

808

429▼

718

143

808

Only countries State Parties to the World Heritage
Convention are labelled on these maps. United Nations
countries boundaries shown as of August 2013.
Twenty-nine properties are nominated and managed by
more than one State Party.

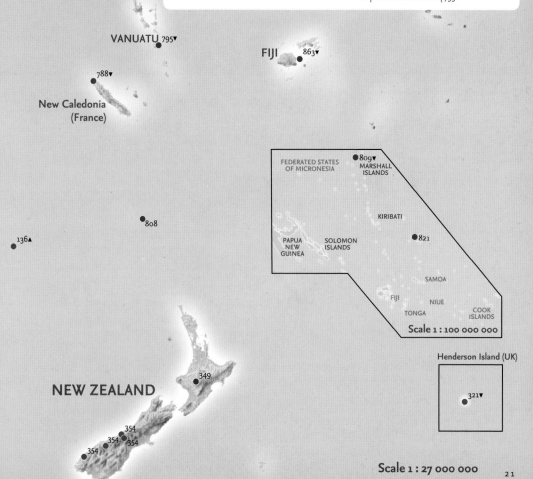

# World Heritage Sites
## Oceania

**Australia**
Australian Convict Sites p808; Australian Fossil Mammal Sites (Riversleigh / Naracoorte) p429▾; Fraser Island p393; Gondwana Rainforests of Australia p260; Great Barrier Reef p122; Greater Blue Mountains Area p609; Heard and McDonald Islands p522▾ (not on map); Kakadu National Park p127; Lord Howe Island Group p136▲; Macquarie Island p506▾ (not on map); Ningaloo Coast p830; Purnululu National Park p699; Royal Exhibition Building and Carlton Gardens p718; Shark Bay, Western Australia p368▲; Sydney Opera House p763; Tasmanian Wilderness p143; Uluru-Kata Tjuta National Park p306; Wet Tropics of Queensland p311; Willandra Lakes Region p125.

**Fiji**
Levuka Historical Port Town p863▾.

**Kiribati**
Phoenix Islands Protected Area p821.

**Marshall Islands**
Bikini Atoll, Nuclear Test Site p809▾.

**New Zealand**
New Zealand Sub-Antarctic Islands p556▲; Te Wahipounamu – South West New Zealand p354; Tongariro National Park p349.

**Palau**
Rock Islands Southern Lagoon p858▾.

**Papua New Guinea**
Kuk Early Agricultural Site p786▲.

**Solomon Islands**
East Rennell p558▾.

**Vanuatu**
Chief Roi Mata's Domain p795▾.

SOLOMON ISLANDS

558▾

VANUATU 795▾

FIJI 863▾

788▾

New Caledonia (France)

FEDERATED STATES OF MICRONESIA

809▾ MARSHALL ISLANDS

KIRIBATI

821

PAPUA NEW GUINEA

SOLOMON ISLANDS

SAMOA

FIJI

NIUE

TONGA

COOK ISLANDS

Scale 1 : 100 000 000

808

136▲

NEW ZEALAND

349

354

354 354

354

556▲

Henderson Island (UK)

321▾

Scale 1 : 27 000 000

KAZAKHSTAN

GEORGIA

ARMENIA

AZERBAIJAN

SEE INSET

IRAQ

KUWAIT

TURKMENISTAN

ISLAMIC REP. OF IRAN

UZBEKISTAN

KYRGYZSTAN

TAJIKISTAN

MON

CH

AFGHANISTAN

SAUDI ARABIA

BAHRAIN

QATAR

UNITED ARAB EMIRATES

OMAN

YEMEN

Socotra (Yemen)

PAKISTAN

NEPAL

BHUTAN

INDIA

BANGLADESH

MYANMAR

MALDIVES

SRI LANKA

601▲ 786▼ 693▼
481▼ 842
435▲ 437▼ 698▲ 557▼ 879▲ 867▲ 867▲
655▼ 500▼ 607▲
837▼ 630▼ 792▲ 767▼ 750▼ 707▲ 729▲ 879▲ 867▲ 867▲ 298▼
761▼ 236 883▲ 815 810▼ 348▼ 879▲ 867▲
215▲ 697▼ 691 746▼ 778▼ 405 670 803▼ 867▲
767▼ 762▼ 835 850▼ 573 629 817▼ 861▼ 425
835 868▲ 846▲ 880▼ 683 703▼ 333▲ 50 576▼ 215▼ 224
88▲ 38▼ 835 110 196 85 222 877▲
798 803▼ 835 835 109▼ 882▲ 765 403 512▼ 576▲ 877▲
820 714 532▼ 576▼ 413 688▼ 877▲
883▼ 849▼ 746▲ 68 835 124 216 161 228
245 864▲ 835 710 102▲ 814▲ 247 154 271▲ 512▼
152 835 118▼ 860▼ 860▼ 249
398▼ 322 760▲ 880▲ 342▲ 183
303 760▲ 730 694▼
614 760▲ 760▲ 156 271▲ 847▼
785▼ 723 160 847▼ 308▲
271▼ 252
237▼ 847▼
576▲ 847▼ 204 7
276
847▼ 138 151▼
363 140
314 823
320 316 877▲

**Inset (SEE INSET):**

SYRIAN ARAB REPUBLIC

LEBANON

ISRAEL
oPt*

JORDAN

Jerusalem

761
569▲ 100
192 191
205 39
197
680 739
793 739
843▼ 105
694▲
875
872▼ 114 221
853 713
739 676
740
212
834

Scale 1 : 12 000 000

*occupied Palestinian territory

Jammu and Kashmir: Dotted line represents approximately the Line of Control in Jammu and Kashmir agreed upon by India and Pakistan. The final status of Jammu and Kashmir has not been agreed upon by the parties.

Only countries States Parties to the World Heritage Convention are labelled on these maps. United Nations countries boundaries shown as of August 2013.

Twenty-nine properties are nominated and managed by more than one State Party.

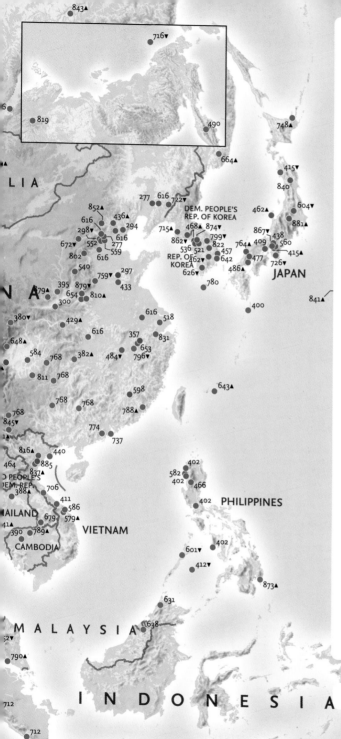

# World Heritage Sites
## Asia, Middle East and Arabian Peninsula

**Afghanistan**
Cultural Landscape and Archaeological Remains of the Bamiyan Valley p703▼; Minaret and Archaeological Remains of Jam p683.

**Armenia**
Cathedral and Churches of Echmiatsin and the Archaeological Site of Zvartnots p655▼; Monasteries of Haghpat and Sanahin p500; Monastery of Geghard and the Upper Azat Valley p630▼.

**Azerbaijan**
Gobustan Rock Art Cultural Landscape p767▼; Walled City of Baku with the Shirvanshah's Palace and Maiden Tower p607▼.

**Bahrain**
Pearling, Testimony of an Island Economy p849▼; Qal'at al-Bahrain – Ancient Harbour and Capital of Dilmun p746▼.

**Bangladesh**
Historic Mosque City of Bagerhat p228; Ruins of the Buddhist Vihara at Paharpur p222; The Sundarbans p512▼.

**Cambodia**
Angkor p390; Temple of Preah Vihear p789▲.

**China**
Ancient Building Complex in the Wudang Mountains p429▲; Ancient City of Ping Yao p540; Ancient Villages in Southern Anhui – Xidi and Hongcun p653; Capital Cities and Tombs of the Ancient Koguryo Kingdom p722▼; Chengjiang Fossil Site p845▼; China Danxia p811; Classical Gardens of Suzhou p518; Cultural Landscape of Honghe Hani Rice Terraces p861▲; Dazu Rock Carvings p584; Fujian Tulou p788▲; Historic Centre of Macao p737; Historic Ensemble of the Potala Palace, Lhasa p425; Huanglong Scenic and Historic Interest Area p395; Imperial Palaces of the Ming and Qing Dynasties in Beijing and Shenyang p277; Imperial Tombs of the Ming and Qing Dynasties p616; Jiuzhaigou Valley Scenic and Historic Interest Area p380▼; Historic Monuments of Dengfeng, in the 'Centre of Heaven and Earth' p810▲; Kaiping Diaolou and Villages p774; Longmen Grottoes p654; Lushan National Park p484▼; Mausoleum of the First Qin Emperor p300; Mogao Caves p298▲; Mount Emei Scenic Area, including Leshan Giant Buddha Scenic Area p481▲; Mount Huangshan p357; Mount Qingcheng and the Dujiangyan Irrigation System p648▲; Mount Sanqingshan National Park p796▼; Mount Taishan p297; Mount Wutai p802; Mount Wuyi p598; Mountain Resort and its Outlying Temples, Chengde p436▲; Old Town of Lijiang p510; Peking Man Site at Zhoukoudian p298▼; Sichuan Giant Panda Sanctuaries – Wolong, Mt Siguniang and Jiajin Mountains p751; Site of Xanadu p852▲; South China Karst p768; Summer Palace and Imperial Garden in Beijing p552; Temple and Cemetery of Confucius and the Kong Family Mansion in Qufu p433; Temple of Heaven: an Imperial Sacrificial Altar in Beijing p559; The Great Wall p294; Three Parallel Rivers of Yunnan Protected Areas p700; West Lake Cultural Landscape of Hangzhou p831; Wulingyuan Scenic and Historic Interest Area p382▲; Xinjiang Tianshan p867▲; Yin Xu p759▼; Yungang Grottoes p672▼.

continued on page 24

Scale 1 : 38 000 000

23

## Georgia
Bagrati Cathedral and Gelati Monastery p435▼; Historical Monuments of Mtskheta p437; Upper Svaneti p481▼.

## India
Agra Fort p161; Ajanta Caves p156; Buddhist Monuments at Sanchi p342▲; Champaner-Pavagadh Archaeological Park p730; Chhatrapati Shivaji Terminus (formerly Victoria Terminus) p723; Churches and Convents of Goa p237▲; Elephanta Caves p271▼; Ellora Caves p160; Fatehpur Sikri p247; Great Living Chola Temples p276; Group of Monuments at Hampi p252; Group of Monuments at Mahabalipuram p204; Group of Monuments at Pattadakal p308▲; Hill Forts of Rajasthan p860▲; Humayun's Tomb, Delhi p403; Jantar Mantar p814▲; Kaziranga National Park p224; Keoladeo National Park p216; Khajuraho Group of Monuments p249; Mahabodhi Temple Complex at Bodh Gaya p688▼; Manas Wildlife Sanctuary p215▼; Mountain Railways of India p576▲; Nanda Devi and Valley of Flowers National Parks p333▲; Qutb Minar and its Monuments, Delhi p413; Red Fort Complex p765; Rock Shelters of Bhimbetka p694▼; Sun Temple, Konârak p183; Sundarbans National Park p271▲; Taj Mahal p154; Western Ghats p847▼.

## Indonesia
Borobudur Temple Compounds p376; Cultural Landscape of Bali Province: the Subak System as a Manifestation of the 'Tri Hita Karana' Philosophy p859; Komodo National Park p370; Lorentz National Park p604▲; Prambanan Temple Compounds p373; Sangiran Early Man Site p503▼; Tropical Rainforest Heritage of Sumatra p712; Ujung Kulon National Park p374▼.

## Iran, Islamic Republic of
Armenian Monastic Ensembles of Iran p792; Bam and its Cultural Landscape p710; Bisotun p762▼; Golestan Palace p868▲; Gonbad-e Qābus p850▼; Masjed-e Jāmé of Isfahan p846; Meidan Emam, Esfahan p38▼; Pasargadae p792; Persepolis p165; Sheikh Safi al-Din Khānegāh and Shrine Ensemble in Ardabil p810▼; Shushtar Historical Hydraulic System p803▲; Soltaniyeh p746▲; Tabriz Historic Bazaar Complex p815; Takht-e Soleyman p691; Tchogha Zanbil p88▲; The Persian Garden p835▼.

## Iraq
Ashur (Qal'at Sherqat) p697▲; Hatra p215▲; Samarra Archaeological City p767▲.

## Israel
Bahá'í Holy Places in Haifa and the Western Galilee p793; Biblical Tels – Megiddo, Hazor, Beer Sheba p739; Incense Route – Desert Cities in the Negev p740; Masada p676; Old City of Acre p680; Sites of Human Evolution at Mount Carmel: The Nahal Me'arot/Wadi el-Mughara Caves p843▼; The White City of Tel-Aviv – The Modern Movement p694▲.

## Japan
Buddhist Monuments in the Horyu-ji Area p415▲; Fujisan, Sacred Place and Source of Artistic Inspiration p867▼; Gusuku Sites and Related Properties of the Kingdom of Ryukyu p643▲; Himeji-jo p409; Hiraizumi – Temples, Gardens and Archaeological Sites Representing the Buddhist Pure Land p840; Hiroshima Peace Memorial (Genbaku Dome) p477; Historic Monuments of Ancient Kyoto (Kyoto, Uji and Otsu Cities) p438; Historic Monuments of Ancient Nara p560; Historic Villages of Shirakawa-go and Gokayama p462▲; Itsukushima Shinto Shrine p486▲; Iwami Ginzan Silver Mine and its Cultural Landscape p764▲; Ogasawara Islands p841▲; Sacred Sites and Pilgrimage Routes in the Kii Mountain Range p726▼; Shirakami-Sanchi p415▼; Shiretoko p748▲; Shrines and Temples of Nikko p604▼; Yakushima p400.

## Jerusalem (Site proposed by Jordan)
Old City of Jerusalem and its Walls p114.

## Jordan
Petra p212; Quseir Amra p221; Um er-Rasas (Kastrom Mefa'a) p713; Wadi Rum Protected Area p834▼.

## Kazakhstan
Mausoleum of Khoja Ahmed Yasawi p707▲; Petroglyphs within the Archaeological Landscape of Tamgaly p729▲; Saryarka – Steppe and Lakes of Northern Kazakhstan p786▼.

## Korea, Democratic People's Republic of
Complex of Koguryo Tombs p715▲; Historic Monuments and Sites in Kaesŏng p862▼.

## Korea, Republic of
Changdeokgung Palace Complex p521; Gochang, Hwasun and Ganghwa Dolmen Sites p626▼; Gyeongju Historic Areas p642; Haeinsa Temple Janggyeong Panjeon, the Depositories for the Tripitaka Koreana Woodblocks p462▼; Historic Villages of Korea: Hahoe and Yangdong p822; Hwaseong Fortress p536; Jeju Volcanic Island and Lava Tubes p780; Jongmyo Shrine p468▲; Royal Tombs of the Joseon Dynasty p799▼; Seokguram Grotto and Bulguksa Temple p457.

## Kyrgyzstan
Sulaiman-Too Sacred Mountain p803▼.

## Lao People's Democratic Republic (Laos)
Town of Luang Prabang p464; Vat Phou and Associated Ancient Settlements within the Champasak Cultural Landscape p679.

## Lebanon
Anjar p205; Baalbek p191; Byblos p192; Ouadi Qadisha (the Holy Valley) and the Forest of the Cedars of God (Horsh Arz el-Rab) p569▲; Tyre p197.

## Malaysia
Archaeological Heritage of the Lenggong Valley p852▼; Gunung Mulu National Park p638; Kinabalu Park p631▲; Melaka and George Town, Historic Cities of the Straits of Malacca p790▲.

## Mongolia
Orkhon Valley Cultural Landscape p719▲; Petroglyphic Complexes of the Mongolian Altai p842; Uus Nuur Basin p693▼.

## Nepal
Chitwan National Park p196; Kathmandu Valley p50; Lumbini, the Birthplace of the Lord Buddha p512▲; Sagarmatha National Park p85.

## Oman
Aflaj Irrigation Systems of Oman p760▲; Archaeological sites of Bat, Al-Khutm and Al-Ayn p322; Bahla Fort p303; Land of Frankincense p614.

## Pakistan
Archaeological Ruins at Moenjodaro p102▲; Buddhist Ruins of Takht-i-Bahi and Neighbouring City Remains at Sahr-i-Bahlol p110; Fort and Shalamar Gardens in Lahore p124; Historic Monuments at Makli, Thatta p118▼; Rohtas Fort p532▼; Taxila p109▼.

## Palestine (oPt) Member of UNESCO since 23 Nov 2011
Birthplace of Jesus: Church of the Nativity and the Pilgrimage Route, Bethlehem p853.

## Philippines
Baroque Churches of the Philippines p402; Historic Town of Vigan p582; Puerto-Princesa Subterranean River National Park p601▼; Rice Terraces of the Philippine Cordilleras p466; Tubbataha Reefs Natural Park p412▼.

## Qatar
Al Zubarah Archaeological Site p864▲.

## Russian Federation (see also p12)
Central Sikhote-Alin p664▲; Citadel, Ancient City and Fortress Buildings of Derbent p698▲; Golden Mountains of Altai p557▲; Lake Baikal p476; Lena Pillars Nature Park p843▲; Natural System of Wrangel Island Reserve p716▼; Putorana Plateau p819; Uus Nuur Basin p693▼; Volcanoes of Kamchatka p490; Western Caucasus p601▲.

## Saudi Arabia
Al-Hijr Archaeological Site (Madâin Sâlih) p798; At Turaif District in ad-Dir'iyah p820.

## Sri Lanka
Ancient City of Polonnaruwa p140; Ancient City of Sigiriya p151▼; Golden Temple of Dambulla p363; Central Highlands of Sri Lanka p823; Old Town of Galle and its Fortifications p320; Sacred City of Anuradhapura p138; Sacred City of Kandy p314; Sinharaja Forest Reserve p316.

## Syrian Arab Republic (Syria)
Ancient City of Aleppo p236; Ancient City of Bosra p105; Ancient City of Damascus p39; Ancient Villages of Northern Syria p837▼; Crac des Chevaliers and Qal'at Salah El-Din p761; Site of Palmyra p100.

## Tajikistan
Proto-urban Site of Sarazm p817▼; Tajik National Park (Mountains of the Pamirs) p861▼.

## Thailand
Ban Chiang Archaeological Site p388▲; Dong Phayayen-Khao Yai Forest Complex p741▲; Historic City of Ayutthaya p359; Historic Town of Sukhothai and Associated Historic Towns p375; Thungyai-Huai Kha Khaeng Wildlife Sanctuaries p364.

## Turkmenistan
Kunya-Urgench p750▲; Parthian Fortresses of Nisa p778▲; State Historical and Cultural Park 'Ancient Merv' p573.

## United Arab Emirates
Cultural Sites of Al Ain (Hafit, Hili, Bidaa Bint Saud and Oases Areas) p835▲.

## Uzbekistan
Historic Centre of Bukhara p405; Historic Centre of Shakhrisyabz p629; Itchan Kala p348▼; Samarkand – Crossroad of Cultures p670.

## Vietnam
Citadel of the Ho Dynasty p837▲; Complex of Hué Monuments p411; Ha Long Bay p440; Hoi An Ancient Town p586; Central Sector of the Imperial Citadel of Thang Long - Hanoi, p816▲; My Son Sanctuary p579▲; Phong Nha-Ke Bang National Park p706.

## Yemen
Historic Town of Zabid p398▲; Old City of Sana'a p245; Old Walled City of Shibam p152; Socotra Archipelago p785▲.

The World Heritage sites,
ordered by the year they were
first inscribed on the List.

# Galápagos Islands
## Ecuador

Criteria – Natural phenomena or beauty; Major stages of Earth's history; Significant ecological and biological processes; Significant natural habitat for biodiversity

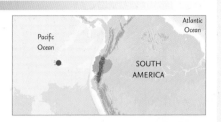

An endemic ▶ Galápagos giant tortoise. Adults in the wild can grow up to 1.2 m in length and live for 150 years. There are now only eleven subspecies remaining from the original twelve.

Situated in the Pacific Ocean approximately 1,000 km from the South American mainland, the Galápagos Archipelago of nineteen major islands and their marine reserve have been called a unique 'living museum and showcase of evolution'. Located at the confluence of three ocean currents, the Galápagos are a 'tossed salad' of marine species.

Volcanic processes formed the islands, most of which are volcanic summits, some rising over 3,000 m from the Pacific floor. They vary greatly in altitude, area and orientation and these differences, combined with their physical separation, contributed towards the species diversity and endemism on particular islands. Ongoing seismic and volcanic activity reflects the processes that formed the islands and it was these processes, together with the islands' extreme isolation, that led to the development of unusual animal life – such as the marine iguana, the giant tortoise and the flightless cormorant – that inspired Charles Darwin's theory of evolution following his visit in 1835.

The western part of the archipelago experiences intense volcanic and seismic activity. The larger islands typically comprise at least one gently sloping shield volcano, culminating in collapsed craters or calderas.

Long stretches of shoreline are only slightly eroded, but in many places faulting and marine erosion have produced steep cliffs and lava, coral or shell sand beaches.

There is coastal vegetation along beaches, salt-water lagoons and low, broken, boulder-strewn shores, and mangrove swamps dominate protected coves and lagoons. The arid zone that lies immediately inland dominates the Galápagos landscape. The humid zone emerges above the arid zone through a transition belt in which elements of the two are combined. It is very damp and is maintained in the dry season by thick, garua fogs. A fern-grass-sedge zone covers the summit areas of the larger islands where moisture is retained in temporary pools.

The endemic fauna includes invertebrate, reptile, marine and bird species. There are a few indigenous mammals. All the reptiles, except for two marine turtles, are endemic.

Marine environments are highly varied and are associated with water temperature regimes reflecting differences in nutrient and light levels. These range from warm temperate conditions brought on by vigorous upwelling (Cromwell Current) and a moderately cool, warm temperate-subtropical influence (Peru Flow).

A Sally Lightfoot ▶ (Graspus Graspus) crab which is endemic to the Galápagos Islands and lives on the rocky shore, feeding on algae and dead fish, birds and seals.

The Heritage site is situated on the Galápagos Submarine Platform and consists of about 120 islands in total. The larger islands in the group are Isabela, Santa Cruz, Fernandina, Santiago and San Cristobal.